Saved By The Son In The Morning Dawn

Kristin Estilow

BookLeaf Publishing

Presentation by *BookLeaf Publishing*

Web: www.bookleafpub.com

E-mail: info@bookleafpub.com

ISBN: 9789357441155

First edition 2023

I'd like to dedicate this book to the Lord Jesus Christ. He should take the credit!

ACKNOWLEDGEMENT

I'd like to thank my friends in music and not in music!! Thank you guys for inspiring me to do what I do. Keep being interesting! Love you guys!! I'd also like to thank my parents because they taught me about Jesus growing up. They are also supportive of my music. My sister too!! Love you fam!!

PREFACE

I decided to write this book as a way for listeners of my music to connect with my lyrics, the writing process, and faith!!

This book is actually geared to those who have not yet found God, but are searching for a Greater Love!! Be the first to see lyrics that may pop up in future songs!!

January (Part 1)

On tour for 6 months
N' now I'm back home again
N' now I'm writing a record
About how this story began

My coffee is in my cup
N' I'm thinkin' bout remember when
Now the sun's down and the trees are dead
And we're back to January again

January
Ooh
January
When the autumn leaves
And the birds and the bees
Are gone to sleep
January
Ooh
January
When everything feels gone before it's begun

But everything gets better
When you see a beacon of light
N' January's a beginning
To the February romantic life

And March has it's flowers
And April has it's showers
And May is actually when it's rainy all day
And June is the Summer
And July it's even warmer
And August has the blazing Sun
And Hopefully at some point you were won
By Jesus Christ the Good Lord’s Son

January (PT 2)-No More January Gloom

January ain't so bad
When ur dancing up on your bed
And you've had too much chocolate on ur spoon

Just let go
Of thoughts in your head
I know you thought that you were so sad
Until you heard a whisper
Jesus in the room

No more
January Gloom

God's Love (D.D. Jackson Gospel Remix) (Part 1)

All you said is that-cha needed someone
To show you love
And that's what I've got
But all you told me
Is that you really cared
But no-one ever really cared
No-one ever really cared

You didn't say it with that typical talk
But I can tell just by the way that you look
Whoah ooh
I'm gonna tell you one thing boy

You need God's Love
Yes you need God's Love
Yes you need God's lovin' boy

God's Love (D.D. Jackson Gospel Remix) (Part 2)

Don't try to tell me I don't know what I'm talkin' about
Don't try to tell me it's not the way
No nooo
Cause I know in your eyes I see whatchu really feelin'
N' I know whatcha feelin'
N' watcha needin' is a different type a love

He needs God's Love
Yes he does
He needs God's Love
Baby

You didn't say it with that typical talk
But I can tell just by the way that you look
Baby
I'm gonna tell you one thing boy

You need God's Love
Yes you need God's Love
Yes you need God's lovin' boy

All you need is God's Love

Yes you need God's Love
Yes you need God's lovin' boy

And there's nothing in this world
That can stop me from showin' you
God's Love

New Year

New Year
Wondering where to go
What to do
Who to hang with
What's the truth

But God knows
Even in your darkest days
When you work too hard
But ur underpaid

When your dreams seem brighter
Than the days
When the hour's later
Than the sun rays

When the World is angry and fighting it out
God has a plan
He's already worked it out

Paradise (Part 1)

Things are not the way they used to be
In the world for you and me
It seems like everything we used to know
Are the places that we cannot go

I've got that feelin'
Got that feelin' (Whoah)
That you've been dreamin'
You been dreamin' (Whoah)
You need a healin'
Need a healin'
(Yeah..heah..heah)
To come out of this
Out of this

Just close your eyes
Just close your eyes
Everything is gonna be alright
Just close your eyes
Just close your eyes
One day you and me will be in Paradise

Paradise (Part 2)

God he's got a plan for you and I
Go to sleep baby please do not cry
And know that you are resting in the Father's
arms
And baby he will keep you strong

I've got that feelin'
Got that feelin' (Whoah)
That you've been dreamin'
You been dreamin' (Whoah)
You need a healin'
Need a healin'
(Yeah..heah..heah)
To come out of this
Out of this

Just close your eyes
Just close your eyes
Everything is gonna be alright
Just close your eyes
Just close your eyes
One day you and me will be in Paradise

Yeah, yeah, yeah
I know that we are in the wake of a storm

But don't worry baby
Jesus will take us home

Just close your eyes
Everything is gonna be alright
Yeah, yeah, yeah
Just close your eyes
Just close your eyes
One day you and me will be in Paradise

Yeah, yeah, yeah
Just close your eyes
Just close your eyes
Everything is gonna be alright
Yeah, yeah, yeah
Just close your eyes
Just close your eyes
One day you and me will be in Paradise

Yeah, Yeah, Yeah
Just close your eyes
Just close your eyes
Everything is gonna be alright
Yeah, yeah, yeah
Just close your eyes
Just close your eyes
One day you and me will be in Paradise

Yeah, yeah, yeah

Just close your eyes
Just close your eyes
Everything is gonna be alright
Yeah, yeah, yeah
Just close your eyes
Just close your eyes
One day you and me will be in Paradise

Yeah, yeah, yeah
Just close your eyes
Just close your eyes

Heaven In Your Eyes

I think I saw heaven
This one time
Or something like it
When I looked in your eyes

Brooks with bridges
Bright colors melding in the sky

Just like a painting
A land better than fantasy
You know
But ask God
I'm sure he can tell you better than me

Here + Now (Believe)-(Part 1)

I need you to believe in a miracle
Oh
I need you to believe
In something spiritual
Oh
I need you to believe
God is the only one
I'm talking Father and The Son

I need you to believe he's the right way
I need you to believe it today
I need you to believe in what I see
Because things need to change

And I say
If u don't know him now
You should really get to know him
And the time is here and now

And I pray
What will it be
Will u do
Do it for me
Accept God

Cuz u n me
Will believe

Here + Now (Believe)-(Part 2)

Hope
Don't give up hope
Hope it surrounds you
Hope
Don't give up hope
Hope he's around you
Peace
Don't give up his peace
Peace he is in u
Peace
Don't give up peace
Peace he will win u

I believe that I've tried and I've tried to tell u
Ooh
I believe that I've told u a thousand times
Oh no
But I know in my heart that I don't have to tell u no more
I believe it's what you are lookin' for
Uh huh

And I say
If u don't know him now

You should really get to know him
And the time is here and now

And I pray
What will it be
Will u do
Do it for me
Accept God
Cuz u n me
Will believe

Believe
Believe
Believe
Uh huh
Yeh yeh
Believe believe believe

Your Calling

There is a shift in the room
The atmosphere is clear
No more dark
No more dreer

A brand new day is finally here
No more crying
In despair
God was always there

Now you finally care
God knows it all
Let his plan turn u here

Down this road
Let him lead the way
It's your calling
Who your supposed to be
Today

Plan 4 U (Remix)(Pt. 1)

When u wake up in the morning with a lot on your mind
N' it seems like u pressed fast forward
But who pressed rewind
The coffee's on the table
N' the complex cut the cable
But u don't have the time
Cuz u know you've got a lot to do

He remembers the first day He met you
He knew you
You were right
Don't you worry baby He won't forget you
And everything's gonna be alright

Oh God
He's got a plan for your life
He won't leave u alone
He will stay by ur side
Oh God
He's gonna take u right thru
Baby listen to me
Cuz baby God's got a plan for u

Plan 4 U Remix (Pt. 2)

The moon looks like it's perfect for you tonight
The stars look like their shinin' just like ur eyes
The planes are flyin' by
High in the sky
And I only wish u knew

He remembers the first day He met you
He knew you
You were right
Don't you worry baby He won't forget you
And everything's gonna be alright

Oh God
He's got a plan for your life
He won't leave u alone
He will stay by ur side
Oh God
He's gonna take u right thru
Baby listen to me
Cuz baby God's got a plan for u

Oh God
He's got a plan for your life
He won't leave u alone
He will stay by ur side

Oh God
He's gonna take u right thru
Baby listen to me
Cuz baby God's got a plan for u

Oh God
He's got a plan for your life
He won't leave u alone
He will stay by ur side
Oh God
He's gonna take u right thru
Baby listen to me
Cuz baby God's got a plan for u

The Game

Ask God
What he wants you to do
Don't you realize
It's not really up to you
He already set a plan
He knows your next move
He knows whether you win or lose
But to win you gotta play right
There is only one way
He knows how to play right
So just ask God if you don't know
If you lose the game, you lose your soul

Prayer Is The Key

Years ago I prayed about this
Miracles they really exist
Talked to God
Said you were worth it
But I didn't know
That Jesus meant this

I saw the light
And baby won't you believe it shines so bright
Wasn't a dream
And baby what do u know now you believe

Ohh
Ur the one that God wants
Ur the one that he needs
He's got you on lock
But baby prayer is the key
Ohh
I've known it for so long
When baby ur next to me
The reason for this song
N' they play you on repeat

It's a rainy day
But all I have to say

Are things will go your way
I know
I know
Clouds are in the sky
But baby now's the time
When you will see the light
I know I know

I saw the light
And baby won't you believe it shines so bright
Wasn't a dream
And baby what do u know now you believe

Ohh
Ur the one that God wants
Ur the one that he needs
He's got you on lock
But baby prayer is the key
Ohh
I've known it for so long
When baby ur next to me
The reason for this song
N' they play you on repeat

Now I see the sunshine
Peaking through the clouds
Baby look now
Baby look now
Oooh

Ur the one that God wants
Ur the one that he needs
He's got you on lock
But baby prayer is the key
Ohh
I've known it for so long
When baby ur next to me
The reason for this song
N' they play you on repeat

Ohh
Ur the one that God wants
Ur the one that he needs
He's got you on lock
But baby prayer is the key
Ohh
I've known it for so long
When baby ur next to me
The reason for this song
N' they play you on repeat

Dreams Come True

Cuz I
Still have faith in you
And I know today
May be the day
That ur dreams come true

Saturday
And I'm in my house
Just thinkin' bout the way
Things are gonna change
And I feel so sure
That God is about to open up the door

All I Need

When you
You don't care anymore
N' ur knocking on his door
And u have faith
And the breath
That you breath in
And u just wanna win
He'll forgive ur sins
N' u have faith

N'
You'll have the victory
When u say that he lives in me
When you fall
When you fall
When u fall on your knees and you pray

Sayin'
I belong to him
He forgave all my sins
Prayer it was the key
Sayin'
Thank you God
Ur all I need

La la la la la la la
La la la la la la la la
La la la la la la
La la la la la la
U've been through so much
Over the past decade
Or more
You've knocked on every door
Oh you tried
You've tried
You tried
Everything
But you finally found what u were lookin' for

N'
You'll have the victory
When u say that he lives in me
When you fall
When you fall
When u fall on your knees and you pray

Sayin'
I belong to him
He forgave all my sins
Prayer it was the key
Sayin'
Thank you God
Ur all I need

La la la la la la la
La la la la la la la la
La la la la la la
La la la la la la

Oh God
U just laid down before him
And poured out ur love u had to give
U don't have an answer to the questions in ur head
But u only have ur love to give

N'
You'll have the victory
When u say that he lives in me
When you fall
When you fall
When u fall on your knees and you pray

Sayin'
I belong to him
He forgave all my sins
Prayer it was the key
Sayin'
Thank you God
Ur all I need

La la la la la la la
La la la la la la la la

La la la la la la
La la la la la la la

God's A Healer

God's a healer
Spring shines
Last year
Hard times
Getting better
Feeling strong
Don't worry babe
He's got it all

Plan 4 U

Change
A change will come
From beginning to the end my friend
The change has to be done

Oh God
He's got a plan for your life
He won't leave u alone
He will stay by ur side
Oh God
He's gonna take u right thru
Baby listen to me
Cuz baby God's got a plan for u

Ooo ooo
I know you really want to
I know you really want to change change
Change change whoah

Change
A change will come
From beginning to the end my friend
The change has to be done

Oh God

He’s got a plan for your life
He won’t leave u alone
He will stay by ur side
Oh God
He’s gonna take u right thru
Baby listen to me
Cuz baby God’s got a plan for u

Ooo ooo
I know you really want to
I know you really want to change change
Change change whoah

Oooo oo
Ooo oo oo
Oo oo ooo oo ooo oo ooo oo oo oo ooo
Ooo ooo
Oo ooo ooo

Ooo
Oo oo oo oo oo oo oo ooo

Smile

Don't lose your smile
Forgetting your joy
God still loves you
Boy

Even if you messed up
1,000 times
He's still waiting
Won't leave you behind

If you take the time
To accept him as Christ
And that he died for your sins

All you have to do is let him in
Let him in
Let him in

Ask forgiveness
For your sins
Ask him into your heart

The Holy Spirit
You can't wait to feel it
He will show you who you are

He will show you who he is
Billion Dollar Smile
Best part about you
It's brighter than ever since

Since now you found the morning star..And
Jesus is the morning star
And everything about you is God made
God made you who you are

Don't be conflicted baby
You've come this far
I'm so proud of the changes
Keep being who you are

In Christ

Conflicted

U wouldn’t know what to do if they left you
If they left u
Out in the cold
Don’t forget he
He will lead you
He will save u
Ur soul

Ur conflicted
At the crossroads
At the crossroads
Of these times
Ur so conflicted
At the crossroads
At the crossroads
Of these times

Oooh
Oh whoa
Ooh whoa
Oh no

U wouldn’t know what to do if they left you
If they left u
Out in the cold

Don’t forget he
He will lead you
He will save u
Ur soul

Cuz ur conflicted
At the crossroads
At the crossroads
Of these times
Ur so conflicted
At the crossroads
At the crossroads
Of these times

Oooh
Oh whoa
Ooh whoa
Oh no

Ur Conflicted
So conflicted
Ur conflicted
So conflicted
Woah
Ur conflicted
So conflicted
Ur conflicted
So conflicted
Whoah

Ur conflicted
At the crossroads
At the crossroads
Of these times
Ur so conflicted
At the crossroads
At the crossroads
Of these times

Oooh
Oh whoa
Ooh whoa
Oh no

Oooh
Oh whoa
Ooh whoa
Oh no

Don’t Be Conflicted, Baby
Be Blessed!!

www.ingramcontent.com/pod-product-compliance
Lightning Source LLC
Chambersburg PA
CBHW051742130826
49812CB00033B/973
9789357441155